A Light Heart Lives Long

By Kathy Davis

Cover Art By: Kathy Davis
Compiled By: Kathy Davis
Edited By: Debbie Hansen
Typeset and Design By: Caroline Solarski and
Julie Otlewis

———

Copyright 1993 Great Quotations Publishing

Published in Glendale Heights by Great Quotations Publishing.
1967 Quincy Court, Glendale Heights, Il 60139

ISBN 1-56245-074-3

Printed in Hong Kong

To the "Big Dog"
Thanks for always being there for me

A light heart lives long.

— Irish Proverb

Trees often transplanted
seldom prosper.

— Dutch Proverb

~~~

Sparrows who emulate peacocks
are likely to break a thigh.

— Burmese Proverb

Don't judge any man
until you have walked two moons
in his moccasins.

— American Indian Proverb

~~~

No one knows what he can do
until he tries.

— Latin Proverb

There is no one as deaf
as he who will not listen.

— Yiddish Proverb

~~~

A friend to everyone and to nobody
is the same thing.

— Origin Unknown

The noisiest drum
has nothing in it but air.

— English Proverb

Go home and make a net
if you desire to get fishes.

— Chinese Proverb

~~~

If love be timid
it is not true.

— Spanish Proverb

A worn path is the safest.

— Latin Proverb

~~~

The greater the fear,
the nearer the danger.

— Origin Unknown

Unshared joy is an unlighted candle.

— Spanish Proverb

~~~

Giving advice to a fool
is like giving medicine to a dead man.

— American Proverb

God gives every bird its food
but does not always
drop it into the nest.

— Danish Proverb

Do not choose for anyone what you do not choose for yourself.

— Persian proverb

~~~

Speaking without thinking is like shooting without taking aim.

— English Proverb

It is better in times of need to have a friend rather than money.

— Greek Proverb

~~~

Cast dirt into the well that gives you water.

— Origin Unknown

He who is shipwrecked a second time
cannot lay the blame on Neptune.

— English Proverb

~~~

That the birds of worry and care
fly above your head,
this you cannot change...
but that they build nests in your hair,
this you can prevent.

— Chinese Proverb

The loftiest towers
rise from the ground.

— Chinese Proverb

As you do to others,
they will do to you.

— Maltese proverb.

~~~

Beauty without grace
is a violet without scent.

— Origin Unknown

You don't water a camel with a spoon.

— Armenian Proverb

~~~

A life without love
is like a year without summer.

— Swedish Proverb

Birds of a feather flock together.

— Latin Proverb

~~~

The four worst things:
a sore head, a bitter tongue,
a troubled mind, and an empty pocket.

— Irish Proverb

The crab instructs its young
" Walk straight ahead like me."

— Hindustani Proverb

If you're well situated, don't move.

— Yiddish Proverb

~~~

When in doubt, don't.

— American Proverb

Little children, little joys;
bigger children, bigger sorrows.

— Yiddish Proverb

~~~

A good name keeps its brightness
even in dark days.

— Latin Proverb

The tongue is not steel — yet it cuts.

—Origin Unknown

~~~

When the fruit is scarce
its taste is sweetest.

— Irish Proverb

A pig grabs the best apple.

— Yiddish Proverb

An inch of gold
will not buy an inch of time.

— Chinese Proverb

~~~

Wit without discretion
is a sword in the hand of a fool.

— Spanish Proverb

Ideas should be clear
and chocolate thick.

— Origin Unknown

~~~

To understand your parents' love
you must raise children yourself.

— Chinese Proverb

Friendship is love with understanding.

— Origin Unknown

~~~

Speed is only good for catching flies.

— Yiddish Proverb

One cannot manage too many affairs;
like pumpkins in the water,
one pops up
while you try to hold down the other.

— Chinese Proverb

Daylight will peep through a very small hole.

— Japanese Proverb

~~~

A wise man hears one word and understands two.

— Yiddish Proverb

With lies you may go ahead in the world
but you can never go back.

— Russian Proverb

~~~

One pound of learning
takes ten pounds of common sense to apply it.

— Persian Proverb

The forest shapes the tree.

— French Proverb

~~~

Birds of prey do not sing.

— German Proverb

The road to a friend's house is never long.

— Danish Proverb

When one isn't hungry,
all soup tastes sour.

— German Proverb

~~~

A drowning man is not troubled by rain.

— Persian Proverb

To mouse there is no greater
beast than cat.

— Armenian Proverb

~~~

If a man knew where he would fall,
he would spread straw there first.

— Finnish Proverb

Even a small thorn causes pain.

— Irish Proverb

~~~

From fortune to misfortune is a short step;
from misfortune to fortune is a long way.

— Yiddish Proverb

When an elephant is in trouble, even a frog will kick him.

— Hindu Proverb

Bake as long as the oven is hot.

— Yiddish Proverb

~~~

He who inherits a penny
is expected to spend a dollar.

— German Proverb

One arrow does not bring down two birds.

— Turkish Proverb

~~~

Truth will always come to the surface.

— Spanish Proverb

It is no use going to the goat's house
to look for wool.

— Irish Proverb

~~~

Eavesdroppers never hear
any good of themselves.

— French Proverb

All is not cream
that comes from a cow.

— Yiddish Proverb

The rich would have to eat money,
but luckily the poor provide food.

— Russian Proverb

~~~

When the heart is full,
the eyes overflow.

— Yiddish Proverb

Many seek good nights and lose good days.

— Dutch Proverb

~~~

Two shorten the road.

— Irish Proverb

There is no one luckier than he who thinks himself so.

— German Proverb

~~~

All that glitters is not gold.

— French Proverb

In a good apple
you sometimes find a worm.

— Yiddish Proverb

Little and often fills the purse.

— German Proverb

~~~

There is no worse water
than standing water.

— French Proverb

Well begun is half done.

— Latin Proverb

~~~

The mills of God grind slowly
but they grind finely.

— Irish Proverb

The truth may walk around naked;
the lie has to be clothed.

— Yiddish Proverb

~~~

The remedy for injuries
is not to remember them.

— German Proverb

It is better to light a candle
than to curse the darkness.

— Chinese Proverb

Drop by drop fills the tub.

— French Proverb

~~~

A man shows his character
by what he laughs at.

— German Proverb

It is not a secret
if it is known by three people.

— Irish Proverb

~~~

A rose too often smelled
loses its fragrance.

— Spanish Proverb.

One meets his destiny
often on the road he takes to avoid it.

— French Proverb

~~~

One enemy can harm you more
than a hundred friends can do you good.

— German Proverb

A single arrow is easily broken, but not ten in a bundle.

— Japanese proverb

Without oars you cannot cross in a boat.

— Japanese Proverb

~~~

Those who are once found to be bad
are presumed to be so forever.

— Latin Proverb

If you try to cleanse others,
you will waste away like soap in the process.

— Madagascan Proverb

~~~

When money speaks,
the truth keeps silent.

— Russian Proverb

There is nothing new under the sun.

— French Proverb

~~~

The just path is always the right one.

— Yiddish Proverb

Coffee should be black as hell,
strong as death, and sweet as love.

— Turkish Proverb

There are many preachers
who don't hear themselves.

— German Proverb

~~~

A liar never believes anyone else.

— Yiddish Proverb

He who would make a fool of himself
finds many to help him.

— Danish Proverb

~~~

To fall down you manage alone
but it takes friendly hands to get up.

— Yiddish Proverb

A lock is better than suspicion.

— Irish Proverb

~~~

Diligence is the mother of good luck.

— French Proverb.

A broken hand works,
but not a broken heart.

— Persian Proverb

Anger should be robbed of its weapon,
not given one.

— Latin Proverb

~~~

Not the cry, but the flight of the wild duck.
leads the flock to fly and follow.

— Chinese Proverb

He who sings frightens away his ills.

— Spanish Proverb

~~~

A word of kindness is better than a fat pie.

— Russian Proverb

He that finds faults wants to buy.

— German Proverb

~~~

It's a good horse that draws its own cart.

— Irish Proverb

Govern a family
as you would cook small fish —
very gently.

— Chinese Proverb

He knocks boldly who brings good news.

— Greek Proverb

~~~

No road is long with good company.

— Turkish Proverb

If everyone gives one thread,
the poor man will have a shirt.

— Russian Proverb

~~~

To worry about tomorrow
is to be unhappy today.

— Turkish Proverb

The three best things:
a little seed in good soil,
a few cows in good grass,
a few friends in the tavern.

— Irish Proverb

~~~

To be a parent takes knowhow,
but everyone takes it on anyhow.

— Yiddish Proverb

He fishes on who catches one.

— French Proverb

You can only find out by trying.

— Greek Proverb

~~~

A wise man has long ears,
big eyes and a short tongue.

— Russian Proverb

As the old bird sings,
the young ones twitter.

— Origin Unknown

~~~

There is no better looking glass
than an old friend.

— Hindu Proverb

We always weaken what we exaggerate.

— French Proverb

~~~

It's the deed that matters, not the fame.

— German Proverb

Praise the children
and they will blossom.

— Irish Proverb

You can't carry two watermelons
in one hand.

— Armenian Proverb

~~~

A piece of bread in the pocket
is better than a feather in the hat.

— Swedish Proverb

That which is loved is always beautiful.

— Norwegian Proverb

~~~

Better to ask twice
than to lose your way once.

— Danish Proverb

It is the heaviest ear of grain
that bends its head the lowest.

— Irish Proverb

~~~

Don't look for applause
until you have cause.

— Yiddish Proverb

He that chases two frogs will catch neither.

— Armenian Proverb

Pride in children
is more precious than money.

— Yiddish Proverb

~~~

He that conceals his grief
finds no remedy for it.

— Turkish Proverb

A friend's eye is a good mirror.

— Irish Proverb

~~~

He who praises little things
is worthy of great ones.

— German Proverb

To know the road ahead,
ask those coming back.

— Chinese Proverb

~~~

He who believes he is deceiving others
often deceives himself.

— French Proverb

A bit of fragrance always clings
to the hand that gives you roses.

— Chinese Proverb

To turn an obstacle to one's advantage
is a great step towards victory.

— French Proverb

~~~

Good health and good sense
are two great blessings.

— Latin Proverb

Patience is a bitter plant
but it has sweet fruit.

— German Proverb

~~~

Ask God for as much as you like
but keep your spade in your hand.

— Armenian Proverb

He that will have the fruit must climb the tree.

— Greek Proverb

One always thinks
that others are happy.

— Yiddish Proverb

~~~

What breaks in a moment
may take years to mend.

— Swedish Proverb

He who holds the ladder
is as bad as the thief.

— German Proverb

~~~

It is a rough road
that leads to the heights of greatness.

— Latin Proverb

To believe everything is too much,
to believe nothing is not enough.

— German Proverb

~~~

If you can't bite,
don't show your teeth.

— Yiddish Proverb

It is good everywhere,
but home is better.

— Yiddish Proverb

God did not create hurry.

— Finnish Proverb

~~~

With one hand he feeds the hens,
with the other he searches for eggs.

— Armenian Proverb

The goat prefers one goat
to a herd of sheep.

— Armenian Proverb

~~~

What is the use of running
when you're not on the right road.

— German Proverb

The worst things:
To be in bed and sleep not.
To want for one who comes not.
To try to please and please not.

— Egyptian Proverb

~~~

Although it rains,
cast not away the watering pot.

— Malaysian Proverb

Better a hen in the hand
than an eagle in the sky.

— Yiddish Proverb

To think is to converse with oneself.

— Spanish Proverb

~~~

There is nothing so bad
that good will not come of it.

— Spanish Proverb

The belly rules the mind.

— Latin Proverb

~~~

The gem cannot be polished without friction,
nor the man perfected without trials.

— Chinese Proverb

Good bargains empty our pockets.

— German Proverb

~~~

Deviate an inch, lose a thousand miles.

- Chinese Proverb

It takes time to build a castle.

— Irish Proverb

One cannot learn to swim in a field.

— Spanish Proverb

~~~

If you are patient in one moment of anger,
you will escape a hundred days of sorrow.

— Chinese Proverb

All sunshine makes a desert.

— Arabian Proverb

~~~

Words should be weighed,
not counted.

— Yiddish Proverb

If you are reluctant to take the way,
you will be lost.

— Malaysian Proverb

~~~

He who wants a rose
must respect the thorn.

— Persian Proverb

Up jumps the rabbit
where you least expect it.

— Spanish Proverb

A mile walked with a friend
contains only a hundred steps.

— Russian Proverb

~~~

The shortest answer is in the doing.

— Greek Proverb

A small minded person
looks at the sky through a reed.

— Japanese Proverb

~~~

Envy and love are opposite principles.

— Greek Proverb

Friends and wine should be old.

— Spanish Proverb

~~~

One thing today, another tomorrow.

— German Proverb

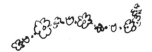

To possess ideas is to gather flowers,
to think is to weave them into garlands.

— Greek Proverb

Even the hen lifts her head toward the heavens
when swallowing her grain.

— African Proverb

~~~

Wishes never filled the bag.

— Greek Proverb

A ragged colt may make a good horse.

— Hindu Proverb

~~~

I not only speak so that I can be understood,
but so that I cannot be misunderstood.

— Origin Unknown

If a fool drops a stone in the well,
forty wise men couldn't draw it out.

— Armenian Proverb

~~~

Only the still pool reflects the stars.

— Chinese Proverb

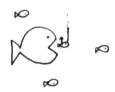

One must lose a minnow
to catch a salmon.

— French Proverb

When the fox cannot reach the grapes
he says they are not ripe.

— Greek Proverb

~~~

They conquer who believe they can.

— Latin Proverb

Patience is the key of joy,
but haste is the key to sorrow.

— Arabian Proverb

~~~

Many take by the bushel
and give by the spoon.

— German Proverb

If you want good service, serve yourself.

— Spanish Proverb

~~~

Good words are like a string of pearls.

— Chinese Proverb

The sun shines brighter
after a shower.

— Yiddish Proverb

Listen to the sound of the river
and you will catch a trout.

— Irish Proverb

~~~

He who has two masters has to lie to one.

— Portuguese Proverb

Much wealth will not come
if a little does not go.

— Chinese Proverb

~~~

You can hardly make a friend in a year,
but you can easily offend one in an hour.

— Chinese Proverb

If you go to war, pray once,
if you go to sea, pray twice,
but pray three times
when you are going to be married.

— Russian Proverb

~~~

Be content with the strength you've got.

— Arabic Proverb

Celebrations have to be made, troubles come by themselves.

— Yiddish Proverb

The cat catches the bird that sings too early.

— German Proverb

~~~

A star, however willing, cannot help the moon.

— Chinese Proverb

Lights of a thousand stars
do not make one moon.

— Chinese Proverb

~~~

The heart of the giver
makes the gift dear and precious.

— Origin Unknown

Show him death and he'll be content with fever.

— Persian Proverb

~~~

One person's owl is another's nightingale.

— German Proverb

Every short dog is bold
in the doorway of its own house.

— Irish Proverb

The glory is not in never failing,
but rising every time you fail.

— Chinese Proverb

~~~

Make your bargain before beginning to plow.

— Arabic Proverb

Only the wearer knows where the shoe pinches.

— English Proverb

~~~

Much is expected where much is given.

— Origin Unknown

Danger and delight grow on one stalk.

— English Proverb

~~~

The bigger a man's head,
the worse his headache.

— Persian Proverb

When the mouse laughs at the cat
there is a hole nearby.

— Nigerean Proverb

Hold a true friend with both your hands.

— Nigerian Proverb

~~~

A wise man changes his mind, a fool never will.

— Spanish Proverb

He who once burnt his mouth
always blows his soup.

— German Proverb

~~~

It is only at the tree loaded with fruit
that the people throw stones.

— French Proverb

Make thyself a sheep
and the wolf is ready.

— Russian Proverb

Everyone must row with the oars he has.

— English Proverb

~~~

He who begins too much accomplishes little.

— German Proverb

Experience is a comb that nature gives us when we are bald.

— Chinese Proverb

~~~

Children are a poor man's riches.

— English Proverb

Trifles make perfection,
but perfection is not trifle.

— Italian Proverb

~~~

A guest sees more in an hour
than the host in a year.

— Polish Proverb

Exaggeration is to paint a snake and add legs.

— Origin Unknown

Necessity is the mother of invention.

— Irish Proverb

~~~

Every man is a master in his own house.

— German Proverb

The way in which something is given
is worth more than the gift itself.

— French Proverb

~~~

God takes notice of clean hands,
not full hands.

— Latin Proverb

The fish that escaped
is the big one.

— Chinese Proverb

Those who know when they have enough
are rich.

— Chinese Proverb

~~~

Better to idle well
than to work badly.

— Spanish Proverb

Gossip is worse than fighting.

— Arabic Proverb

~~~

If you don't crack the shell,
you can't eat the nut.

— Russian Proverb

Everybody loves the tree
which gives him shelter.

— Russian Proverb

~~~

Promises may get friends,
but it is performances that keeps them.

— Origin Unknown

He who laugh

— Norwegian

~~

Experience wit
is better than learning

— American

As the old birds sing,
the young ones twitter.

— Origin Unknown

The sky is
whe

No on
to do wi

Do not cut down the tree
that gives you shade.

— Arabian Proverb

If you stop every time a dog barks,
your road will never end.

— Arabian Proverb

~~~

Joy and sorrow are next door neighbors.

— German Proverb

He who builds to everyman's advice
will have a crooked house.

— Danish Proverb

~~~

A bird can roost on but one branch.

— Chinese proverb

Better an empty purse than an empty head.

— German Proverb

~~~

Life is half spent before one knows what life is.

— French Proverb

Trumpet in a herd of elephants,
bleat in a flock of goats,
crow in the company of cocks.

— Malaysian Proverb

The mind covers more ground than the heart
but goes less far.

— Chinese Proverb

~~~

The toe of the star gazer is often stubbed.

— Russian Proverb

Men trip not on mountains,
they stumble on stones.

— Hindustani Proverb

~~~

If a little tree grows
in the shade of a larger tree,
it will die small.

— Origin unknown

However big the whale may be,
a tiny harpoon can rob him of life.

— Malaysian Proverb

Between saying and doing
many a pair of shoes is worn out.

— Italian Proverb

~~~

Advice after injury
is like medicine after death.

— Danish Proverb

Life is the greatest bargain,
we got it for nothing.

— Yiddish Proverb

~~~

Wisdom and virtue
are like two wheels of a cart.

— Japanese Proverb

He who does not know one thing
knows another.

— Kenyan Proverb

~~~

Rain beats a leopard's skin,
but it does not wash out the spots.

— Ashanti Proverb

He who gifts to me teaches me to give.

— Danish Proverb

God shares with the person that is generous.

— Irish Proverb

~~~

A good conscience is a soft pillow.

— German Proverb

One may go a long way after he is tired.

— French Proverb

~~~

That which is bitter to endure
may be sweet to remember.

— Latin Proverb

The journey of a thousand miles
starts with a single step.

— Chinese Proverb

~~~

Better to be slow than rash.

— Spanish Proverb

Everyone can navigate
in fine weather.

— Italian Proverb

They can concur who believe they can.

— Greek Proverb

~~~

Use not the sword
against him who asks forgiveness.

— Turkish Proverb

Wonder is the beginning of wisdom.

— Greek Proverb

~~~

What the wind brings it will also take away.

— Armenian Proverb

Worry often gives a small thing a big shadow.

— Swedish Proverb

~~~

Don't look for bargains
and you won't be disappointed.

— Yiddish Proverb

As long as the sun shines,
one does not ask for the moon.

— Russian Proverb

Tell not all you know,
believe not all you hear,
do not all you are able.

— Italian Proverb

~~~

To question a wise man
is the beginning of wisdom.

— German Proverb

Don't try to fly before you have wings.

— French Proverb

~~~

Make sure to be in with your own equals
if you're going to fall out with your superiors.

— Yiddish Proverb

If you sit in a hot bath
you think the whole town is warm.

— Yiddish Proverb

A prudent man
does not make the goat his gardener.

— Hungarian Proverb

~~~

Every man knows good counsel
except him that has need of it.

— German Proverb

If pulled in one direction,
the world would keel over.

— Yiddish Proverb

~~~

If you take big paces,
you leave big spaces.

— Burmese Proverb

If each one sweeps before his own door,
the whole street will be clean.

— Yiddish Proverb

He who would leap must take a long run.

— Danish Proverb

~~~

The camel does not see his own hump.

— Armenian Proverb

One cannot both feast and become rich.

— Ashanti Proverb

~~~

When the moon is not full,
the stars shine more brightly.

— Buganda Proverb

The riches that are in the heart
cannot be stolen.

— Russian Proverb